IMAGES
of America

JEFFERSON CITY AT WAR
1916–1975

Although the Jefferson City National Cemetery was not officially established until 1867, burials of Union soldiers during the Civil War occurred as early as 1861. This is the cemetery gate at the East McCarty Street entrance. (Courtesy of Shawn C. Johnson.)

On the Cover: On November 11, 1921, in the House of Representatives chamber at the state capitol, Gov. Arthur M. Hyde signs the Soldier's Bonus Bill and then presents it to the soldiers of Missouri, represented by Ed Arnett, a Missouri National Guardsman and World War I veteran, and other members of American Legion Post 5. The bill authorized the issuance of $15 million in bonds to cover cash payments to the state's World War I veterans. Governor Hyde became the secretary of agriculture under Pres. Herbert Hoover in 1929. (Courtesy of American Legion Post 5.)

IMAGES
of America

JEFFERSON CITY AT WAR
1916–1975

Jeremy P. Amick

ARCADIA
PUBLISHING

ISBN 978-1-4671-1159-1

Published by Arcadia Publishing
Charleston, South Carolina

Printed in the United States of America

Library of Congress Control Number: 2013949025

For all general information, please contact Arcadia Publishing:
Telephone 843-853-2070
Fax 843-853-0044
E-mail sales@arcadiapublishing.com
For customer service and orders:
Toll-Free 1-888-313-2665

Visit us on the Internet at www.arcadiapublishing.com

I must first thank my Lord Jesus Christ, through whom all things are possible. Secondly, my wife, Tina, for indulging me with large amounts of patience and support while I immersed myself in this patriotic and eye-opening endeavor. Finally, for all veterans past and present—without whose sacrifice this book would never have been possible.

Contents

ACKNOWLEDGMENTS

I cannot extend enough appreciation for the expertise and assistance of my friend Shawn C. Johnson, who has a keen eye for a good photograph and who has been by my side in virtually every opportunity to honor and recognize our fellow veterans. I am also thankful for the assistance of the Missouri State Museum, the Museum of Missouri Military History, American Legion Post 5, Veterans of Foreign Wars Post 1003, and the Central Missouri Detachment of the Marine Corps League, for digging into their archives for historical military photographs of the Jefferson City community. I am thankful as well for individuals such as Harold Markway, Mary Frank, Bill Stine, and Larry Schepker, who actively assisted me in locating numerous photographs for this project.

INTRODUCTION

After Missouri became the 24th state to enter the union, on August 10, 1821, several years passed before the City of Jefferson was established as the official seat of state government, heralded by the completion of the first capitol building in 1826. In the succeeding years, the community began to flourish as the river town established its economic footing and businesses and borders expanded. But the relatively peaceful climate enjoyed throughout the early decades of the city's existence was not destined to last, and war soon interrupted the daily routines, leading to innumerable men being pulled from their personal endeavors and thrust into the bloody conflict known as the Civil War.

Scores of songs, books, television shows, and movies have chronicled not only the impact this war had on the entire nation, but, more specifically, the consequences it had for Missouri and its towns, including Jefferson City. Yet, as is well documented in firsthand accounts written during the period, which are available through the Missouri State Museum, the hardy fighting spirit of these Missourians prevailed, and difficult times were overcome. This has served as a lesson for subsequent generations regarding the impact such conflicts can have within a community. Despite this overarching effect of the Civil War, later struggles unfolded for which local men and women sacrificed their time and, occasionally, their lives, in support of a cause they believed to be greater than themselves. The years, however, continued their grind forward and whittled away many of the firsthand recollections of service that occurred outside of the span of the Civil War, which have often faded from the public memory.

Were it not for the photographs taken from Jefferson City resident and National Guardsman Clifford Porth (who later assumed ownership of the business founded by his father, Porth's Jewelry, on High Street), many Jefferson City residents would be unaware of the past service of a National Guard unit once headquartered in the city. This photographic chronicle has its origins on June 18, 1916, when Pres. Woodrow Wilson issued an order mobilizing the National Guard in response to raiding parties and other depredations occurring along the United States-Mexico border. Answering the president's call, the Missouri National Guard mobilized 5,030 soldiers under the command of Brig. Gen. Harvey C. Clark. The unit was sent to assist with the border troubles in what would later be recognized as the Mexican Border War.

One of the multiple companies and units from Missouri deployed in support of the president's call was Company L, 2nd Missouri Infantry. The company had been formed in 1897 in Jefferson City, was later disbanded, and was then reorganized in 1909. Many of the soldiers of the company lived and worked in Jefferson City. After returning to their hometown following the war, they often became successful business owners and pillars of the community. Of even greater interest, however, is that, just months after their return from the Mexican border, a large number of the company traveled to Europe to fight in World War I, after the company was federalized into service as a machine-gun company.

In the weeks and months after Armistice Day, local men and women returned home and began to build families and businesses, as had happened following previous conflicts. Unfortunately,

Jefferson City had sacrificed many of its own sons and daughters in support of the war against the Central Powers. Those fortunate enough to return could not have known that, in the coming years, many of their own sons and daughters would be called upon to fight in yet another world war. Some were drafted, some volunteered, but all proudly answered the nation's call to the colors. And, as had been previously done by young men and women of Jefferson City, lives were sacrificed on behalf of their state and nation. Others returned to their homes, working to build a better community and earning respect and adoration by demonstrating in their daily lives the work ethic often refined while they served in the military.

Later decades would see the same spirit of service and sacrifice, as young men and women deployed in support of the Korean War and the Vietnam War. Throughout the years, many brave individuals serving in the armed forces, though not originally from the area, were drawn to the community and chose to relocate to Jefferson City after their discharge. These newcomers inspired in others a level of pride and patriotism that continues to resonate to this day.

This book will help walk the reader through Jefferson City's military history, beginning with the Mexican Border War and continuing through the Vietnam War. Photographs will introduce the reader to the city's rich past and highlight the spirit of volunteerism and dedication demonstrated by those who have donned a uniform in service to city, state, and nation. Welcome to the history of Jefferson City at war.

One

The Mexican Border War and World War I

Members of Company L, 2nd Missouri Infantry, perform bayonet exercises while stationed near Laredo, Texas, during the Mexican Border War. The unit, from Jefferson City, was commanded by local resident Capt. William S. Moore. Clifford Porth, the company's lieutenant and also a Jefferson City resident, chronicled the company's service through scores of photographs, many of which are included in this book. (Missouri State Museum, Missouri State Parks.)

Soldiers in Company L, 2nd Missouri Infantry, train with a machine gun while stationed near the Laredo District in 1916. The district, commanded by Brig. Gen. William A. Mann of the Army, comprised 145 miles of border. (Missouri State Museum, Missouri State Parks.)

This photograph, taken on October 14, 1916, shows Company L troops driving their military vehicles while on patrol duty in San Ygnacio, Texas. Company L was assigned to the area from September 8, 1916, until October 16, 1916, at which time it was relieved by companies of the 4th Missouri Infantry. It then returned to the Laredo District. (Missouri State Museum, Missouri State Parks.)

Soldiers of Company L, 2nd Missouri Infantry, wait in the mess line while on patrol in San Ygnacio, Texas. The company arrived in Laredo, Texas, on July 7, 1916, and continued to support the Mexican Border War efforts until it was relieved from federal service at Fort Riley, Kansas, on January 13, 1917. (Missouri State Museum, Missouri State Parks.)

Members of Company L, 2nd Missouri Infantry, pose for a photograph with a rattlesnake captured in the camp. Company L previously mustered into service in support of the Spanish-American War, along with the entire 2nd Missouri Infantry regiment, on May 6, 1898. The governor had made a call for volunteers in response to the president's request for 200,000 troops from the National Guard. The company never left the United States and mustered out of federal service on March 3, 1899. (Missouri State Museum, Missouri State Parks.)

While stationed near Laredo, Texas, Missouri National Guardsmen stayed in rugged structures like the ones pictured here. (Missouri State Museum, Missouri State Parks.)

Lt. Clifford Porth, seen here in 1916, is credited with having taken numerous photographs of Company L's involvement throughout the conflict. He returned to Jefferson City in early 1917 and, several months later, was one of many of the company's members mobilized for service in World War I. He later took over the operation of Porth's Jewelry, on High Street, a business that was founded by his father, George Porth. (Missouri State Museum, Missouri State Parks.)

The headquarters armory for the state militia (above), built in 1861, was once located on the southwest corner of the state capitol grounds. Behind the building, across Broadway Street and toward the left edge of this photograph, is St. Peter's Catholic Church. (Cole County Historical Society.)

Created by St. Louis sculptor Carl C. Mose, this Spanish-American War monument has stood watch over Jefferson City from its current location on Business 50 (Missouri Boulevard) since 1967. The soldier on the monument, wearing a brimmed hat tipped to the left, an ammunition belt, and a rifle slung over his right shoulder, represents the more than 10,000 Missourians who served in the Spanish-American War, the Boxer Rebellion, and in the Philippines from 1898 to 1902. (Shawn C. Johnson.)

A memorial arch was erected across High Street at the Madison Street intersection for a homecoming parade on October 7, 1919. The parade honored the memory of Cole County's fallen heroes. The wooden arch was constructed by local carpenters with materials donated by the Scruggs-Guhleman Lumber Company. (Cole County Historical Society.)

A young boy stands next to the base of the memorial arch, which lists the names of Cole County residents who lost their lives in World War I. (Cole County Historical Society.)

The line of march for the homecoming parade, led by the 140th Regimental Band of Kansas City, began at the capitol and proceeded down High Street. At the parade's end, at McClung Park, the community held a barbecue, which included entertainment for local service members and their families. Reports indicate that 20,000 county residents turned out for the day's festivities. (James R. Sone.)

The Missouri State Chapter of the American War Mothers dedicated a bronze tablet in the east wing of the Missouri capitol in 1928. The tablet memorializes the service of the "sons and daughters of Missouri in the World War." The American War Mothers is a nonprofit organization founded in 1917 by mothers who had lost children during World War I. The group's congressional charter was changed in later years to extend membership to mothers of children serving, or of those who have served, in the armed forces during a time of conflict. (Jeremy P. Amick.)

Roscoe Enloe was inducted into the Missouri National Guard on June 30, 1917, just shy of his 22nd birthday, and he was assigned to Company L, 2nd Missouri Infantry. The unit was later federalized into service and sent to Europe to fight in World War I, becoming the 130th Machine Battalion. Enloe was killed in action on September 29, 1918, as part of the Meuse-Argonne offensive. He had volunteered to take a position in front of his gun squad to observe the enemy and direct machine-gun fire. (Jeremy P. Amick.)

After volunteering to take a position in front of his gun squad, Roscoe Enloe was shot through the right lung when a German machine gun opened fire on his position. Enloe's twin brother, Robert Enloe, helped drag his wounded brother to safety, but Roscoe died from his injury. (American Legion Post 5.)

Robert Enloe, the twin brother of Roscoe Enloe, was a member of the 130th Machine Gun Battalion. He was present when Roscoe received a fatal gunshot wound during the Meuse-Argonne offensive. Robert was later promoted to the rank of second lieutenant and served with the 815th Pioneer Infantry Regiment until his discharge in July 1919. (American Legion Post 5.)

The older brother of Roscoe and Robert, Dr. Lawrence David Enloe was a local physician and a member of the Medical Corps during World War I. He served with Hospital Unit No. 76 in Vichy, France. This photograph was taken in 1928, when Dr. Enloe served as the commander of American Legion Post 5. (American Legion Post 5.)

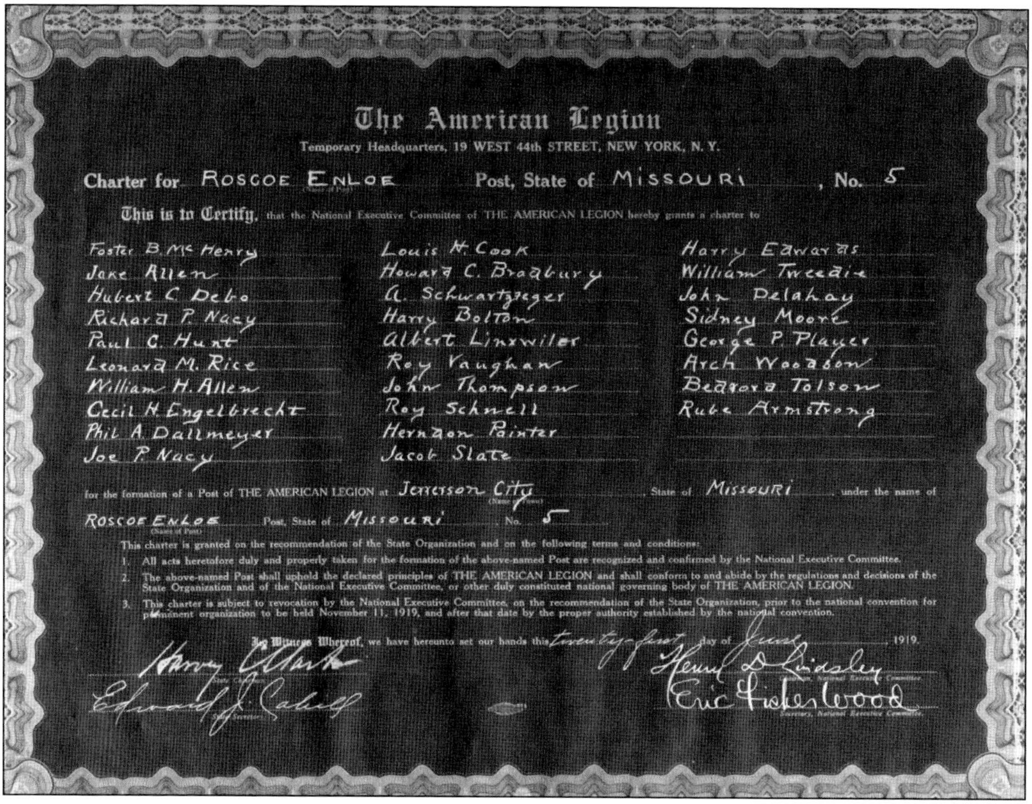

The American Legion

Temporary Headquarters, 19 WEST 44th STREET, NEW YORK, N. Y.

Charter for ROSCOE ENLOE Post, State of MISSOURI, No. 5

This is to Certify, that the National Executive Committee of THE AMERICAN LEGION hereby grants a charter to

Foster B. McHenry	Louis H. Cook	Harry Edwards
Jake Allen	Howard C. Bradbury	William Tweedie
Hubert C. Debo	A. Schwartzreger	John Delahay
Richard P. Nacy	Harry Bolton	Sidney Moore
Paul C. Hunt	Albert Linxwiler	George P. Player
Leonard M. Rice	Roy Vaughan	Arch Woodson
William H. Allen	John Thompson	Bedford Tolson
Cecil H. Engelbrecht	Roy Schnell	Rube Armstrong
Phil A. Dallmeyer	Herndon Painter	
Joe P. Nacy	Jacob Slate	

for the formation of a Post of THE AMERICAN LEGION at Jefferson City, State of Missouri, under the name of ROSCOE ENLOE Post, State of Missouri, No. 5

This charter is granted on the recommendation of the State Organization and on the following terms and conditions:

1. All acts heretofore duly and properly taken for the formation of the above-named Post are recognized and confirmed by the National Executive Committee.
2. The above-named Post shall uphold the declared principles of THE AMERICAN LEGION and shall conform to and abide by the regulations and decisions of the State Organization and of the National Executive Committee, or other duly constituted national governing body of THE AMERICAN LEGION.
3. This charter is subject to revocation by the National Executive Committee, on the recommendation of the State Organization, prior to the national convention for permanent organization to be held November 11, 1919, and after that date by the proper authority established by the national convention.

In Witness Whereof, we have hereunto set our hands this twenty-first day of June, 1919.

Harry Clark, State Chairman

Edward J. Cahill, State Secretary

Henry D. Lindsley, Chairman, National Executive Committee

Eric Fisher Wood, Secretary, National Executive Committee

American Legion Post 5 was established in Jefferson City and named in honor of Cole County resident Roscoe Enloe, who was killed during World War I . The American Legion was founded by veterans of the American Expeditionary Forces in 1919, and Post 5 received its official charter on June 21, 1919. Shown above is a copy of the original charter. (American Legion Post 5.)

Alfred Raithel, pictured here in 1918 eating with full pack and gear, was inducted into the Army on September 20, 1917. The Jefferson City native was initially assigned to Company M, 356th Infantry, 89th Division, and sailed for France on July 31, 1918. He took part in fighting at Lucey, St. Mihiel, and in the Meuse-Argonne offensive. Raithel was transferred to HQ Company, 323rd Infantry, 81st Division, in January 1919. (Gertrude Strobel.)

Alfred Raithel (right) returned to the United States on June 14, 1919, and was discharged from the Army 10 days later. After the war, in 1920, he went to work as assistant manager of the newly founded MFA Exchange in Lohman, Missouri. He went on to serve as manager from 1943 to 1960. Raithel passed away on September 25, 1963, and is buried in the cemetery at St. Paul's Lutheran Church in Lohman. (Gertrude Strobel.)

In 2012, a memorial stone was found discarded in a vacant wooded lot on the west end of Jefferson City. The granite marker is inscribed, "Memory Row Dedicated by American War Mothers for Services 1917–1929." (Shawn C. Johnson.)

It was later discovered that the memorial stone was constructed in honor of the state's military members killed in World War I and had been dedicated in 1929 by American War Mothers and placed in a roadside park. The park was removed when roadway expansion took place to support the Capital Mall, which was built in the late 1970s. The marker is seen here following its rededication and placement near the entrance of Memorial Park. (Shawn C. Johnson.)

After World War I, at the request of the state legislature, several Missouri counties honored the men and women who served with commemorative banners. The banner for Cole County (shown here) was made by the Cole County Court and presented to the state in January 1924, along with 68 banners from other Missouri counties. The upper number represents the number of individuals from the county who served during the war. The number inside the star indicates those from the county who lost their lives while in the service. The Missouri State Museum has approximately 100 of these banners in its collection. (Missouri State Museum, Missouri State Parks.)

This bronze statue of Missouri native Gen. John J. Pershing, commander of the American Expeditionary Forces during World War I, was erected in 1957, four years after the general assembly appropriated $25,000 for its creation. It was placed on the east grounds of the state capitol. In 1968, the monument was relocated to the historic site bearing the general's name in his boyhood hometown of Laclede, Missouri. (Missouri State Archives.)

As a young boy growing up on East Dunklin Street in Jefferson City, Toney Jenkins loved the game of baseball. He earned a reputation in the community as being proficient at the game. On October 29, 1917, the 21-year-old Jenkins was inducted into the Army. He was serving with Company G, 369th Infantry, 92nd Division, when he was killed on September 28, 1918. (American Legion Post 231.)

Toney Jenkins is buried in the Jefferson City National Cemetery. He is believed to have been the only African American service member from the community killed during World War I. In 1934, American Legion Post 231, the second Legion post in Jefferson City, was chartered. It has been a predominantly black post since that time. (Shawn C. Johnson.)

Leslie William Stine, inducted into the Army on April 14, 1918, was initially assigned to the Iowa State College Training Detachment. At this location, draftees were trained as auto mechanics, blacksmiths, or machinists. Stine was later transferred overseas and served with both Battery A, 22nd Field Artillery, and Company B, 53rd Pioneer Infantry Regiment. He was severely wounded in France on October 14, 1918, and later received a Purple Heart. (Bill Stine.)

Harvey Burks was inducted into the Army in October 1916 and participated in several major engagements during World War I. He suffered an attack of pleurisy during his wartime service, which weakened him to the extent that he later succumbed to tuberculosis. He died on April 16, 1924, at the US Veterans Hospital at Jefferson Barracks, Missouri. Several months after Burks's death, his father was awarded a death compensation of $20 a month by the US Veterans Bureau. (Pete Hartman.)

Inducted into the Army in Jefferson City on April 26, 1918, Charles H. Tucker trained at Camp Funston, Kansas, before boarding a ship for Europe on June 4, 1918. Tucker maintained a brief journal chronicling his overseas service, noting time served in trenches and foxholes in several locations throughout France. He also included his time on the front lines during the St. Mihiel drive. He later served as part of the Army of Occupation in Germany. Tucker returned to the United States in May 1919. (Pat Schell.)

This 1920s photograph shows the southwest corner of the Cole County Courthouse and the World War I monument (to the right of the Coca-Cola stand) as it appeared shortly after its erection. The structure, built by Jefferson City monument maker C.G. Mace, was formally dedicated in a ceremony on June 25, 1923. It cost $2,200 to build. (Cole County Historical Society.)

This recent photograph shows the World War I memorial as it looks today. The shaft of the monument was designed with rough granite to symbolize the sturdy character and steadfastness of American troops who served during the war. The memorial was funded through donations from the Rotary Club, women's clubs of the city, and the county court, as well as by interest earned on the memorial fund and money from a state appropriation. (Shawn C. Johnson.)

The memorial tablet (pictured here) and bronze eagle adorning the top of the World War I monument were the work of the St. Louis Brass Company. The tablet listed the names of the 58 county residents killed during the war, including one woman. Jefferson City resident Grace Hershey lost her life at sea while in the service of the American Red Cross. (Shawn C. Johnson.)

Phillip A. Dallmeyer Sr. was inducted into the Army on September 9, 1918, and served with the Commissioned Officers Training School at Camp Pike, Arkansas. (Steve Dallmeyer.)

In 1913, prior to his service during World War I, Phillip A. Dallmeyer Sr. established a watch repair and optical shop in the 200 block of Madison Street. The company would become Dallmeyer's Jewelry, and the operation of the business was taken over by his son, Phillip Dallmeyer Jr., a World War II aviator, in 1946. Dallmeyer Sr. is pictured here in 1931, when he served as commander of American Legion Post 5. (American Legion Post 5.)

Inducted into the service on September 20, 1917, Emil Van Loo served with the Army. He was shot in the left thigh on September 28, 1918, near Verdun, France, and was admitted to the base hospital the following day. Van Loo was discharged from the service at Camp Dodge, Iowa, on April 30, 1919, and later received a disability rating of 50 percent for injuries that continued to trouble him in later years. (Helen Lepage.)

Emil Van Loo (second from right) is shown in a hospital in France in 1918 while recovering from a leg wound he incurred in combat. Following his return from the war, Van Loo, like many area residents, continued his family's agricultural tradition by purchasing his own farm. (Helen Lepage.)

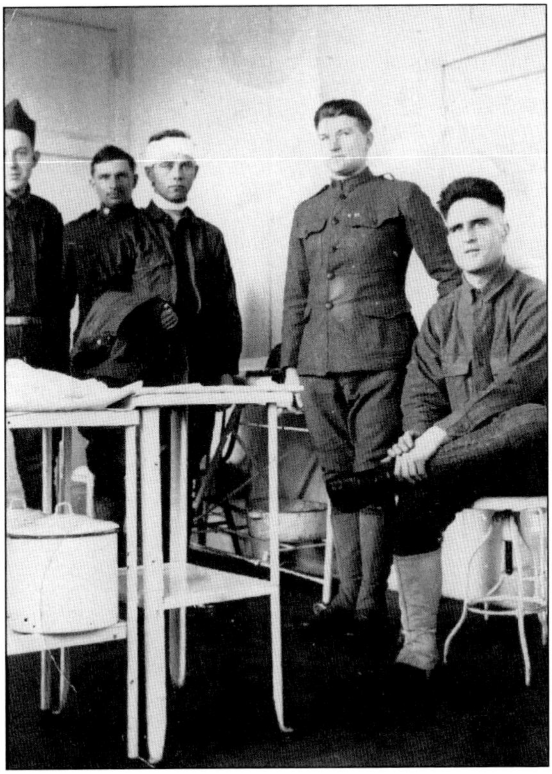

Jefferson City resident Milo Henry Walz was inducted into the Army on February 26, 1918. He went on to serve overseas from June 28, 1918, to January 24, 1919, with the 342nd Field Artillery. (Amy Freeman.)

Armed with only an eighth-grade education, Milo Walz returned from the war and became a very successful businessman in the mid-Missouri area. He opened a furniture store in 1923 on East Dunklin Street in Jefferson City, which later grew into separate furniture, appliance, carpet, drapery, and hardware stores in locations including Columbia, Osage Beach, and Holts Summit. (Amy Freeman.)

Jacob Schepker (right) was born and raised in Jefferson City. He later moved to South Dakota to work on his uncle's farm. From there, he joined the Army on August 28, 1918, serving with Company C, 20th Infantry. While in the service, he died from complications related to pneumonia. (Larry Schepker.)

Edgar T. Tanner, the descendant of well-known Jefferson City businessmen, received schooling to become a dentist after graduating high school. He later had offices in the Central Trust Building. Tanner served during World War I and attained the rank of first lieutenant. (American Legion Post 5.)

Peter Delong, inducted into the Army at St. Louis on June 26, 1918, was initially assigned to the 162nd Depot Brigade. On August 19, 1918, he was transferred to the Mobile Laundry Company, No. 319 QMC, with whom he remained until his discharge. After the war, he was employed as a blacksmith and steel fabricator and worked at Eagan's Machine Shop and Cady's Machine Shop. Delong died in 1990 at the Missouri Veterans Home in Mexico, Missouri. (Larry Schepker.)

Many American Legion posts had drum and bugle corps and rifle teams, which would compete in competitions against other posts. This is the American Legion Post 5 rifle team, which earned the title of state champion in 1932. (American Legion Post 5.)

Members of the American Legion Post 5 drum and bugle corps posed for this photograph during the 1935 American Legion Convention in St. Louis. (American Legion Post 5.)

Lawrence Prenger (seated) and Joseph Markway pose for a photograph in their World War I uniforms. Prenger was inducted into the Army on July 22, 1918, and served with Battery A, 30th Field Artillery. Markway entered service on the same date and served with Battery B, 30th Field Artillery. (Harold Markway.)

Pvt. Roy Sone poses in his Marine Corps uniform in 1917. Sone served with Company 47, 5th Regiment, 2nd Division, during World War I. He was killed in action on October 4, 1918. Veterans of Foreign Wars Post 1003, on East Capitol Avenue, was named in his honor. (VFW Post 1003.)

This portrait of Pvt. Roy Sone was unveiled and dedicated in the Missouri House of Representatives at the state capitol in 1924. Painted by St. Louis artist Charles Brethauer, the portrait was presented to VFW Post 1003. It still hangs in the main room of the post. (Shawn C. Johnson.)

The photograph below, taken on the summit of Mont Blanc Ridge in France, shows the makeshift grave of Pvt. Roy Sone and three of his comrades killed in action. Sone's remains were returned to Jefferson City and interred in Riverview Cemetery on August 14, 1921. (VFW Post 1003.)

Pvt. Roy Sone's gravestone is located in Riverview Cemetery in Jefferson City. Every Memorial Day, VFW Post 1003, along with the Marine Corps League, conducts a ceremony to honor the fallen Marine. (Shawn C. Johnson.)

This photograph, taken around 1916, shows the three Sone brothers with their mother, Leater H. Sone. The brothers are Roy Sone (left), Guy Sone (center), and Bay Sone. Guy volunteered to serve with the Army but was denied enlistment due to asthma. Bay, who served during World War I with the Army, was able to locate his brother's grave on Mount Blanc Ridge in France. (James R. Sone.)

Tom Ward (left) and James Roy Sone, nephew of the post's namesake, stand in front of Veterans of Foreign Wars Post 1003 on East Capitol Avenue. The post has been at its current location since the 1950s, after moving from its previous home on Madison Street. (Shawn C. Johnson.)

Hubert Peter Lauf enlisted in the Army in 1917 and served overseas during World War I with the 355th Ambulance Corps, 89th Division. Graduating law school in 1923, Lauf became an attorney in Jefferson City and later served in the state legislature. The veteran, seen here in 1927, became the commander of Roy Sone VFW Post 1003. He also served as the VFW state commander. Lauf died in 1954. (VFW Post 1003.)

Henry Buehrle served in the Navy during World War I. Returning to Jefferson City, he worked several sales jobs before opening Buehrle's Grocery at the corner of Main Street and Boonville Road in 1936. Buehrle operated the business with his wife and daughter until his death in 1956. (Carolyn Buehrle Brown.)

Thorpe Gordon served overseas with Company B, 337th Machine Battalion. He began his career as an undertaker and, after the war, went on to establish his own funeral home business. Gordon was very involved in the community, serving for 26 years on the Jefferson City School Board. He was an active member of the Rotary Club and the chamber of commerce, and he served two terms as commander of American Legion Post 5. (American Legion Post 5.)

Born on January 20, 1892, Fredolin "Fritz" Buehrle volunteered for the Army during World War I and served as a cook with Company M, 356th Infantry, 89th Division. While in Europe, he was exposed to gas, which later resulted in his contraction of tuberculosis. After the war, Buehrle moved to Arizona to help fight his respiratory ailment, but he later returned to Jefferson City, where he died in 1924 at the age of 32. The local Disabled American Veterans post, Oliver-Buehrle Chapter 17, was co-named in honor of Buehrle's sacrifice. (Bill Stine.)

Two

World War II

Harold Markway is seen in his Navy uniform in 1945. The young sailor was one of the original crewmembers to serve aboard the small destroyer USS *Rowan* during the ship's commissioning in World War II. Markway served his entire time overseas in the Pacific. (Harold Markway.)

Harold Markway is seen above in the early 1950s with the Budweiser Mule Team in front of the C&H Tavern. Shortly after his return from the war, Markway opened the tavern in partnership with his uncle, Charlie Prenger. In 1959, he opened the Wel-Com-Inn on the corner of Madison and West Dunklin Streets. Markway owned and operated the bar until 1982. (Harold Markway.)

In 1943, at the age of 17, Pete Adkins enlisted in the Navy, attending signal school at San Pedro, California, where he learned to communicate with ships using flags and flashing lights denoting Morse code. He was stationed in the Marshall Islands for more than two years during the war and helped direct vessel traffic in and out of harbors while working from a signal tower. Adkins is pictured here at boot camp at Farragut, Idaho, in 1943. (Lorraine Adkins.)

Pete Adkins was discharged from the Navy in 1946 and went on to enjoy a successful career as the head football coach at Jefferson City High School from 1958 to 1995. Over the course of his 37-year career, Adkins compiled a 405-60-4 record. He was inducted into the Missouri Sports Hall of Fame in April 2013. Here, Adkins speaks to his team in a Jefferson City High School locker room in 1966. (Lorraine Adkins.)

During the early part of World War II, Cletus Kramer was working in St. Louis, helping to build the Curtiss C-46 Commando, a transport plane used in the war effort. In 1943, he received a draft notice. His boss told Kramer that he could help him secure a deferment, but Kramer declined the offer and was inducted into the Army Air Corps, becoming a gunner on a B-17 bomber. (Cletus Kramer family.)

Cletus Kramer was based in Foggia, Italy, with the 817th Squadron, 483rd Bomb Group, 15th Air Force. On November 22, 1944, while flying his sixth mission, his B-17 bomber was struck by enemy fire. Kramer evacuated the aircraft and was captured in Austria. He eventually ended up in Stalag Luft IV, near Gross Tychow, Pomerania (now Tychowo, Poland). Kramer remained a prisoner of Germany until he was liberated by Patton's 104th Infantry Division on April 26, 1945. Kramer is standing on the left in this photograph, taken shortly after he was liberated from the prison camp. (Cletus Kramer family.)

Pictured in 2000, Cletus Kramer holds a framed handkerchief sewn with images symbolizing the bomb group he served with and the names and positions of the crewmembers with him the day his B-17 was hit and the crew was forced to evacuate. Kramer sewed the handkerchief while in German prison camps, using embroider hoops fashioned from rims of powdered milk tins, thread from socks and other articles of clothing, and a Red Cross sewing kit. (Cletus Kramer family.)

Female veterans of World War II helped establish Central Missouri Women's Post 496 of Jefferson City. Here, post officers are installed during a special ceremony in the hearing room of the State Highway Building on December 11, 1946. (American Legion Post 5.)

Wesley Godsy was drafted into the Army in February 1944 and, just months later, participated in the D-Day landings at Normandy Beach with soldiers of the 1st Infantry Division. Godsy (left) is seen here in 1945 while serving as a military policeman in Germany with Company L, 26th Infantry, during the Nuremberg Trials. While the trials were taking place, Godsy and fellow soldiers helped guard several war criminals, including field marshal Hermann Goering. (Martin Godsy.)

Known throughout the Jefferson City area for the countless hours he volunteered to church and community organizations, Linus Hohm was always focused on supporting his fellow veterans in any way possible. Hohm served in the Army during the Korean War and later enlisted in the Army Reserves. He was employed with Roark Aluminum and was especially active with Veterans of Foreign Wars Post 1003 and Disabled American Veterans Chapter 17. (Carolyn Schramm.)

Born in Jefferson City in 1927, James Reed attended local schools and was drafted into the Army in April 1945. Following his initial training, Reed was stationed at Kyoto and Kobe, Japan, spending the next year working as a pastry baker and a machinist. He also played guitar in a band that performed at officer and USO functions. (Linda Stolte.)

Marcellus Markway was inducted into the Army at Jefferson Barracks on April 15, 1941. He became a medical technician with Company B, 109th Medical Battalion, 34th Division, and served in several campaigns and battles, including Rome-Arno, Northern Apennines, Po Valley, Tunisian, and Naples-Foggia. Markway earned five Bronze Stars. He was discharged from the Army on July 22, 1945, and returned to Jefferson City, where he became a general contractor and the owner of Markway Construction. (Emily Crawford.)

Standing by the ambulance he used to transport wounded soldiers during World War II, Marcellus Markway (left) learned that, despite the large red crosses painted on the vehicles, the enemy did not always respect the humanitarian charge of the medical corps. Markway's medical company was strafed with 20-millimeter fire from German planes while serving in Africa. Standing here with Markway is local resident Carl DeBroeck. (Emily Crawford.)

Maurice Markway, the twin brother of Marcellus Markway, was inducted into the Army at Fort Leavenworth, Kansas, on June 16, 1941. The following year, Markway was accepted into the Army's aviation division (the Army Air Forces) and completed the training to become a radar operator aboard a B-17. The airman participated in his first bombing mission on December 4, 1944, and flew regular missions until the war in Europe ended the following year. (Emily Crawford.)

On February 3, 1945, while serving as a tail gunner on a B-17 bomber, Ralph Kalberloh's aircraft was shot down near Berlin, Germany. Kalberloh parachuted from the plane and was able to evade capture for five days before surrendering to German authorities after succumbing to hunger. The young airman was held as a prisoner of war by the Germans until April 29, 1945, when he was liberated by American troops under the command of Gen. George Patton. He is seen here in a military photograph taken in Kingman, Arizona, in 1944. (Ralph Kalberloh.)

Taken in 1944 at Biggs Field, Texas, the photograph above shows Ralph Kalberloh with fellow B-17 crewmembers after their return from a simulated bombing mission. They are, from left to right, (first row) Ralph Kalberloh, tail gunner; Fred Eisenlord, flight engineer; and Bill Charliton, radio operator; (second row) Ross Purdy, navigator; Wally Oldham, pilot; Carl Dunn, copilot; and Howard Leach, bombardier. (Ralph Kalberloh.)

Alfred Eiken relaxes in uniform in front of the Missouri capitol about 1943. Eiken enlisted in the Army Air Forces in 1942 and completed bombardier training in Texas the following year. He was later transferred to Tinian, in the Mariana Islands. From this location, the B-29 bomber he was assigned to completed 28 successful missions. Unfortunately, things would later take a turn for the worse. (Donna Boyd.)

On a mission to deliver supplies to prisoners of war in Japan on August 30, 1945, Alfred Eiken (second row, second from right) and 11 of his crewmembers were killed when the wing of their plane clipped a mountain and crashed. The 12 service members were buried in the US Armed Forces Cemetery in Yokohama, Japan. In 1949, Eiken's body was returned to his family and reinterred in the parish cemetery at St. Francis Xavier Catholic Church in Taos, Missouri. (Donna Boyd.)

This local advertisement was typical of notices following the surrender of Germany on May 8, 1945. The nation was encouraged to continue its support of the war effort by the purchase of war bonds. At the same time, such statements provided a warning to Japanese forces. (American Legion Post 5.)

Edward "Babe" Gross graduated from Jefferson City High School in 1938 and went to work for the Curtiss-Wright factory in St. Louis, where he helped build the B-25 Mitchell, a twin-engine bomber. He was drafted into the Army Air Forces in 1943 and trained to become a radio operator aboard the B-25s he had helped build. (Ed Gross.)

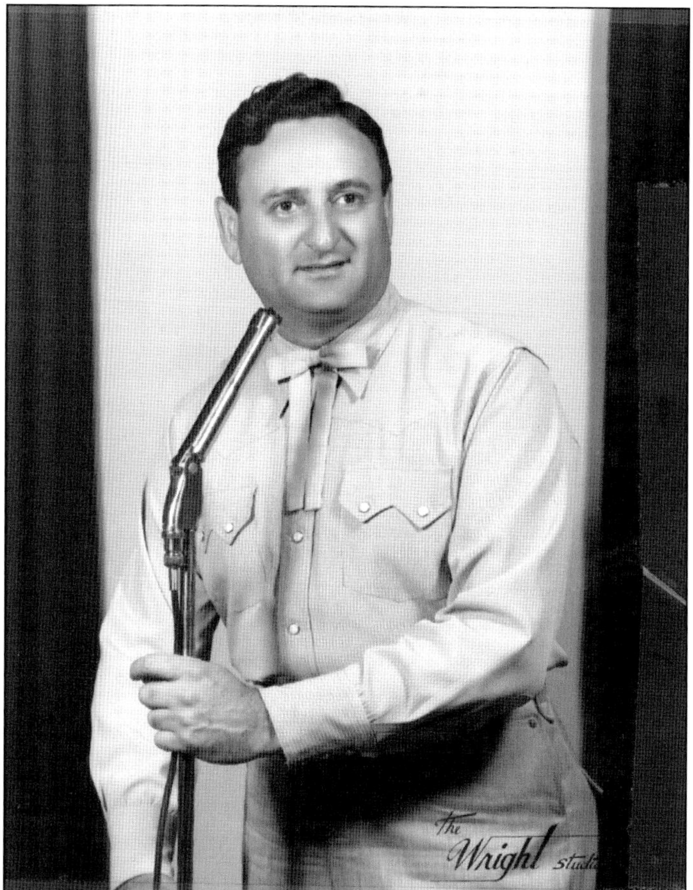

In 1944, Ed Gross (above, left) poses next to the "Plastered Bastard," one of the B-25s he served on as a radio operator and gunner during World War II. He was discharged from the service in 1945, having participated in 72 bombing missions in locations throughout the South Pacific. (Ed Gross.)

After the war, Ed Gross worked full-time for the state highway department. However, his passion was for dance. He became a well-known dance instructor in many mid-Missouri communities. Gross, who also learned to serve as a square-dance caller, is pictured here in his "calling" attire in 1955. (Ed Gross.)

Inducted into the Army in November 1942, James R. McIlwain trained in wire communications and served in locations throughout the Pacific during the war. He is seen here while stationed on the island of New Caledonia in 1943. (Carrie McIlwain.)

Ruth Buell enlisted in the Women Accepted for Volunteer Emergency Service (WAVES) program during World War II. She served in a clerical support role at the Armed Guard Center in Brooklyn, New York, until her discharge in 1946. WAVES was established by the Navy in 1942 to help fill stateside positions left vacant as men were deployed overseas to fight the war. (Ruth Buell.)

Sgt. Robert Buell, pictured here in 1943 while serving as an aircraft mechanic in Italy, was in the Army Air Forces during World War II. Buell initially served with the ground crew of a B-24 Liberator, but later volunteered to become a tail gunner when he was told that he could go home if he survived 50 missions. (Ruth Buell.)

Bob Buell was discharged from the service in 1945 after surviving three plane crashes. He later retired from employment with the State of Missouri. "Bad Bob," as he was affectionately known by his friends, passed away in 2013. (Ruth Buell.)

Enlisting in the Army Air Corps in May 1942, Francis "Bud" Jones went on to become a pilot. He flew 117 combat missions in P-40 Warhawks and P-47 Thunderbolts during the war. (Bud Jones.)

Below, Bud Jones stands next to the P-47 Thunderbolt he was flying when it was hit four times with 20-millimeter cannon fire on September 8, 1944. One of the cannon rounds cracked an engine cylinder and cut the oil line, spraying oil on the plane, including inside the cockpit and on Jones. As a testament to the plane's durability, Jones was able to make the 180-mile trip back to his air base before the engine seized up. (Bud Jones.)

Bud Jones (above) was discharged from the service in 1945 and went on to serve part-time with the Air Force Reserve. He worked full-time for the Missouri State Highway Patrol and retired from both his patrol and his Air Force Reserve careers on the same day: May 12, 1981. He is pictured here in his patrol uniform in the early 1960s, filling in for one of the desk sergeants at the Troop F headquarters in Jefferson City. (Bud Jones.)

Ellsworth Forbis was inducted into the Army in April 1944 and served in the Ardennes, Central Europe, and the Rhineland, earning a Purple Heart on May 12, 1945. After the war, he returned to Jefferson City, where he worked for local companies, eventually retiring from Chesebrough Ponds. (Lesley Gerhart.)

Sam Bushman III joined the Navy in 1940 after graduating from law school at the University of Missouri. Assigned to naval intelligence at Pearl Harbor after December 7, 1941, he requested sea duty and was appointed a gunnery officer aboard the USS *Earl V. Johnson*. Bushman saw duty in North Africa, Leyte (Philippines), and Okinawa. He left the service in 1946 at the rank of lieutenant commander and returned to Jefferson City to practice law. (Sam Bushman IV.)

While serving aboard the USS *Earl V. Johnson* during World War II, Bushman's captain pursued the hobby of photography. In 1944, he helped create Christmas greetings for the sailors to send home to their friends and families. Shown below are Bushman and his wife, Dorothy. (Sam Bushman IV.)

John Sullivan enlisted in the Army Air Corps in May 1942 and was trained as a bombardier and navigator. Assigned to the crew of a B-24 Liberator with the 330th Squadron, 93rd Bombardment Group, 1st Lieutenant Sullivan participated in 35 missions throughout Europe during World War II. He notes that none of his fellow crewmembers were killed or seriously injured. (John L. Sullivan.)

Below, John Sullivan (standing, far right) poses for a photograph next to a B-24 Liberator with his crewmembers in March 1944. The photograph was taken while the group was training on the aircraft at Westover Field in Massachusetts. Weeks later, Sullivan and his crew boarded a troopship, the *Queen Elizabeth*, and traveled overseas, where they were assigned to the 93rd Bombardment Group in Hardwick, England. (John L. Sullivan.)

This is to Certify

that 1ST LT. JOHN L. SULLIVAN of 330 th Squadron, 93rd Bombardment Group (H) A. A. F. has completed with honor to his country, comrades and himself, 35 bombing missions over enemy territory as herewith listed.

1. GIEN	6 JUL 44	18. COULOMMIERS	11 AUG 44
2. PERONNE	8 JUL 44	19. TACT. TAR. FR.	13 AUG 44
3. SAARBRUCKEN	16 JUL 44	20. DIJON/LONGUIC A/F	14 AUG 44
4. GRENTEMVILLE	18 JUL 44	21. WITTMUNDHAFEN	15 AUG 44
5. STRASBOURG	19 JUL 44	22. MAGDABURG	16 AUG 44
6. SCHMALKALDEN	20 JUL 44	23. WILLEBRUCK	25 AUG 44
7. MUNICH	21 JUL 44	24. GROESBEEK	18 SEPT 44
8. LAON ATHES	23 JUL 44	25. KOBLENZ	21 SEPT 44
9. ST. LO AREA	24 JUL 44	26. KASSEL	27 SEPT 44
10. ST. LO AREA	25 JUL 44	27. KASSEL	28 SEPT 44
11. OSCHERSLABEN	29 JUL 44	28. HAMM	2 OCT 44
12. MONTEREAU	2 AUG 44	29. LIPPSTADT	5 OCT 44
13. ROSTOCK	4 AUG 44	30. ZELLERFEILD	7 OCT 44
14. FALLERSLEBEN	5 AUG 44	31. OSNABRUCK	12 OCT 44
15. HEIDE	6 AUG 44	32. KAISERSLAUTERN	14 OCT 44
16 PERONNE	7 AUG 44	33. HAMBURG	30 OCT 44
17. CLASTERES	8 AUG 44	34. MISBURG	4 NOV 44
		35. KARLSRUE	5 NOV 44

Squadron Commander

HARVEY P. BARNARD, JR.,
Colonel, Air Corps,
Commanding.

When discharged from their service with the Army Air Forces in World War II, many aircrew members received documentation outlining the locations and dates of the bombing missions in which they participated. This is the document highlighting the 35 bombing missions that local resident John Sullivan participated in while serving with the 93rd Bombardment Group. (John L. Sullivan.)

As part of a Flag Day program on June 14, 1940, local patriotic and civic groups participated in a parade in downtown Jefferson City. The American Legion Post 5 drum and bugle corps is seen passing the Cole County Courthouse while traveling west on High Street. Members of the highway patrol, the city police, the Missouri National Guard, and the Boy Scouts and Girl Scouts also participated in the event. (American Legion Post 5.)

Above, the Flag Day parade ended on the south side of the Missouri state capitol, where the guests of honor were Jefferson City's War Mothers and Gus Loesch, who, at the time, was 97 years old and the only surviving local soldier of the Civil War. In the foreground is the American Legion's drum and bugle corps. (American Legion Post 5.)

Serving more than two years in Europe during World War II, Gilbert Pritzel, seen here in 1943, participated in the landings at Normandy on D-Day and went on to serve in battles at Naples, Foggia, and the Rhineland, earning five Bronze Stars for valor. In 2010, he was awarded the French Legion of Honor medal by Gov. Jay Nixon during a ceremony at the state capitol. (Judi Hasler.)

Above, members of Wardsville's St. Stanislaus Catholic Church who served during World War II pose for a group photograph in 1946. (Harold Markway.)

Lt. Col. James T. Blair Jr. (right) receives the Legion of Merit in 1944 for helping to organize a group of airborne parachute troops that were part of the Allied assault on D-Day. Blair enlisted in the Army Air Forces in 1942 and served in Europe for three years, participating in night flights from both England and Africa. (Myrna Blair.)

Lt. Col. James T. Blair Jr. (left) visits with Duke Shoop, a reporter for the *Kansas City Star*, when the two met briefly in France during World War II. Prior to the war, Shoop served briefly in Jefferson City as the paper's statehouse correspondent. In 1947, Blair became mayor of Jefferson City. He was elected lieutenant governor two years later, remaining in that office until he became governor of Missouri in 1957. Blair retired from politics in 1961 after completing his term as governor. (Myrna Blair.)

This photograph was taken of Bill McAnany while the young sailor was home on leave in 1941. During his two-decade naval career, McAnany served aboard several hospital ships and provided medical support services during World War II and the Korean War. (Bill McAnany.)

Shown here are, from left to right, Bill McAnany, Jack Hilliard, "Snuffy" Smith, Joe Barnett, and C.G. Johnson. This photograph was taken while the five sailors were enjoying a tour of Oahu on the morning of December 7, 1941. Shortly after the picture was taken, the first wave of attacks against the Navy by Japanese planes began at Pearl Harbor. (Bill McAnany.)

The USS *Solace* was a cruise liner converted to a 400-bed hospital ship during World War II. Bill McAnany was part of the ship's commissioning detail and served onboard as an X-ray technician from August 1941 until November 1943. The *Solace* was moored in Pearl Harbor when the Japanese attacked in December 1941. It later received, treated, and transported to naval hospitals casualties resulting from conflict in Guadalcanal. (Bill McAnany.)

The SS *Jefferson City Victory* was launched on January 30, 1945, and joined the fleet of hundreds of "victory ships" built during World War II to haul cargo for the United States and its allies. The vessel was sold to a private interest in 1949 and was eventually scrapped. (Photograph by Walter E. Frost; courtesy of City of Vancouver Archives.)

Roy Convery (right) entered the Navy on November 4, 1935, and became a career sailor, serving until his retirement on May 29, 1956. He was one day out of Pearl Harbor with a group of carriers transporting planes to Wake Island when the Japanese attack began. He later served in support of Patton's 3rd Army by running boats across the Rhine River into Germany, where he finished out the war. Convery is pictured here in the late 1930s with his father, James (center), and his brother Earl. (James Convery.)

Phillip Dallmeyer Jr. spent a lifetime serving his country and his community. A 1941 graduate of Jefferson City High School, Dallmeyer attended college at the University of Missouri–Columbia and enlisted in the Marine Corps shortly after the United States entered World War II. He piloted both the SBD Dauntless dive-bomber and the FRSU Corsair, and he flew missions from islands in the Pacific against various Japanese targets. (Steve Dallmeyer.)

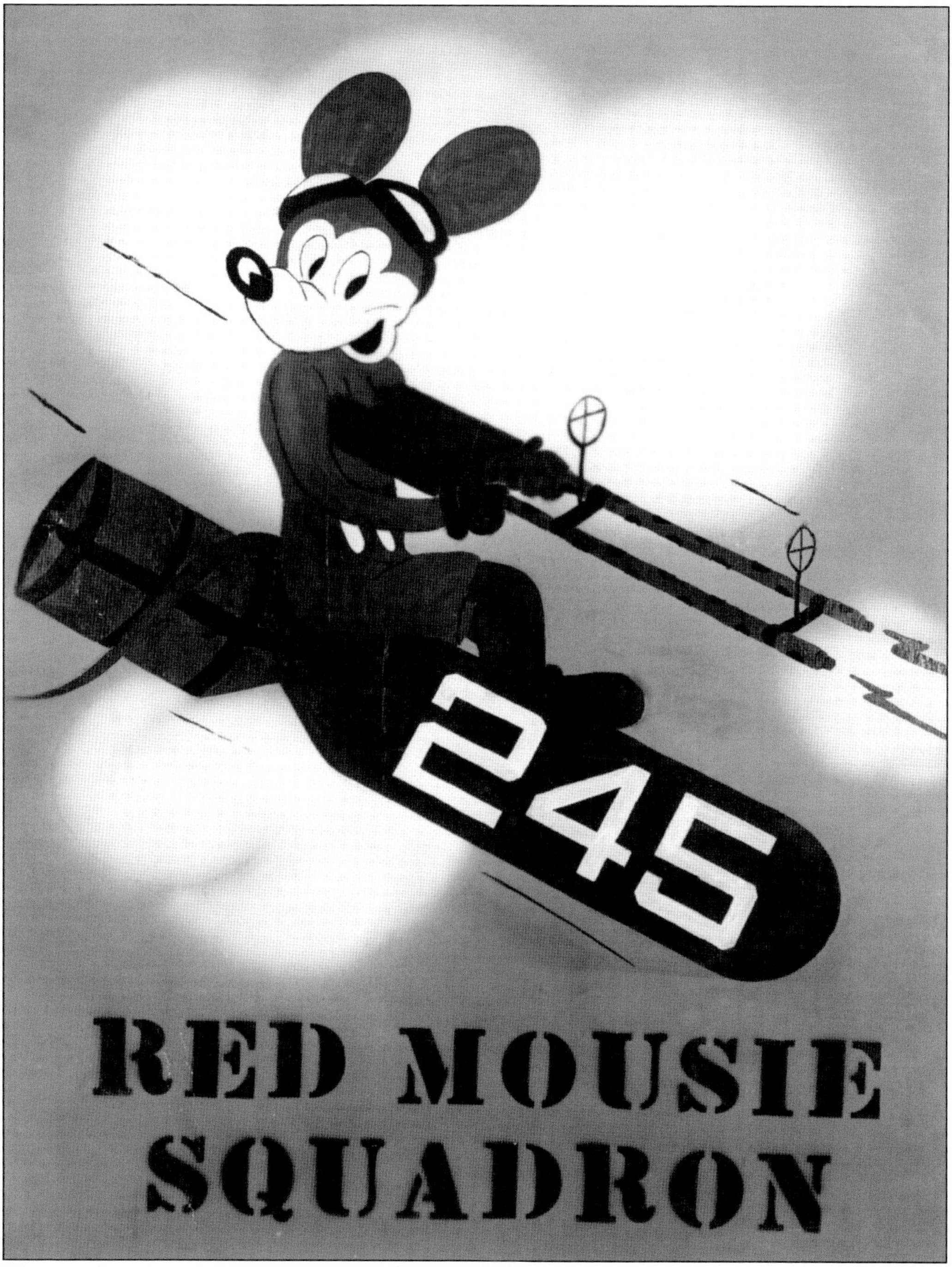

This patch is from Marine Corps Bombing Squadron 243, a dive-bomber squadron to which Phillip Dallmeyer Jr. was assigned during the war. The squadron has been deactivated since November 1945. Following his discharge from active duty in 1946, Dallmeyer became a partner in his father's jewelry business. He served as commandant of the Central Missouri Marine Corps League and commander of American Legion Post 5. He also volunteered with numerous community organizations. (Steve Dallmeyer.)

Sylvester Boehm served as a medic during World War II, attached to the 549th Anti-Aircraft Artillery Battalion. His service during the war included fighting battles in the Ardennes and the Rhineland and liberating the Buchenwald concentration camp. (William Stine.)

Following the surrender of Germany, Pres. Harry S. Truman visited Europe in July 1945. While stationed in Europe with the Army, local resident Sylvester Boehm snapped this photograph of the president traveling in Belgium. (William Stine.)

In a ceremony on November 7, 2011, Missouri governor Jay Nixon (left) presents Wilburn Rowden with a Silver Star Banner in honor of injuries he received during his military combat service. Rowden was drafted into the Army Air Corps in 1943 and served as a radio operator on a B-17 bomber. On his sixth and final mission, Rowden's bomber was shot down by German fighter planes. Rowden was able to evacuate the aircraft, but he was captured by the German military and spent 13 months in prison camps until his liberation by the 104th Division on April 26, 1945. (Shawn C. Johnson.)

Wilburn Rowden was discharged from the service in November 1945 and, several months later, joined the Missouri National Guard. He retired from the National Guard in 1983 at the rank of chief warrant officer four, having dedicated more than 38 years of his life in service to state and country. Rowden is pictured here as a master sergeant in 1970. (Wilburn Rowden.)

The French Legion of Honor, created by Napoleon Bonaparte in 1802, is the country's highest award for extraordinary contributions. World War II veterans are considered for this honor if they participated in one of the three major campaigns involving the liberation of France. (Shawn C. Johnson.)

Lloyd Cain (below, left) is awarded the Silver Star Medal by Brig. Gen. Robinson Duff at Frankfurt, Germany, on July 4, 1947. Cain served with the Army in Europe during World War II. Later, he earned a Purple Heart while serving as a heavy-mortar commander for the 40th Infantry Division, 224th Infantry Regiment, during the Korean War. In 1965, the combat veteran deployed to Vietnam, where he served a one-year stint as a senior Army advisor. He retired in 1976 with 33 years of service. (Lloyd Cain.)

Frank Crooks enlisted in the Army Air Corps in 1943 and completed 60 combat missions as a top turret gunner/engineer on a B-26 Marauder. He later served in the Air National Guard and retired in 1984 after nearly 40 years of service. Due to Crooks's exemplary career in both the enlisted and officer ranks, in August of that year, Gov. Christopher "Kit" Bond used a special authority in Missouri's statutes to promote Crooks—at that time a brigadier general—to the rank of major general, and then placed him on the state's retired list. (Frank Crooks.)

Enlisting in the Marine Corps in September 1942, Wyman S. Basinger fought in several key campaigns in the Pacific during World War II. He was injured twice at Okinawa: first with fragment wounds to his hands, and then with a second, more serious injury to his back from shell fragments. Basinger was discharged on November 9, 1945, but was recalled to active service in 1951 during the Korean War, serving in California until his discharge on August 15, 1952. (Becky Ambrose.)

Wyman Basinger was a member of several local veterans' organizations, including American Legion Post 5, Veterans of Foreign Wars Post 1003, the Disabled American Veterans, and the Marine Corps League. In 1968, he was elected Cole County sheriff. While serving his fifth consecutive term, he died from a massive blood clot in 1986. Basinger is pictured here in his sheriff's uniform around 1985. (Becky Ambrose.)

At 21 years old, Bob Hunter enlisted in the Army Air Corps and, after his basic training, became a flight cadet. He then completed training to become a B-24 bomber pilot and flew 51 missions over Europe, earning a Distinguished Flying Cross for the bombing of the oil refineries and rail yards in Ploesti, Romania, on June 23, 1944. (Becky Ambrose.)

After his return from the war, Bob Hunter went on to serve in the Air Force Reserves and retired at the rank of lieutenant colonel. He was also employed as the chief engineer for the Missouri Highway and Transportation Department, retiring in 1985 after 35 years of service. Hunter is pictured here in 1944 piloting a B-24. (Becky Ambrose.)

Lester Schepker is pictured here with his daughter Mary Leslie and his wife, Marjorie. He was raised in the Jefferson City area and, while growing up, spent time working at Delong's Blacksmith Shop on Jefferson Street. In 1945, at the age of 36, Schepker was inducted into the Army and was stationed in the Philippines, where he served as a military policeman. He was discharged from the service in 1946 and spent several decades working on the road in sales until retiring in 1974 at the age of 65. (Michelle Wiegand.)

Raised on a farm near the west end of Jefferson City, Bernard Schepker was inducted into the Army on September 24, 1944, and served as an air compressor operator with Company B, 836th Engineer Aviation Battalion. While serving in the southern Philippines, Schepker was wounded by shrapnel on May 11, 1945, an injury that earned him a Purple Heart. He is pictured here in 1945 with his sisters Rosaline Distler (left) and Helen Schepker. (Marie Schepker.)

Born in 1922, Jacob Schepker fought with the Marine Corps in the Pacific during World War II. He later cofounded Schepker Brothers Service Company with his brother Bernard in North St. Louis. He was active in many community organizations and local political campaigns. He died on March 2, 2010, and is buried at Jefferson Barracks National Cemetery. (Stanley Schepker.)

Karl Bennett, who grew up in Jefferson City, enlisted in the Marine Corps on January 12, 1942. He served in the Pacific with the 3rd Division, participating in landings and combat in locations including Guadalcanal, Guam, and Iwo Jima. He was discharged from the Marines at Norfolk, Virginia, on October 26, 1945. (Tim Bennett.)

Vincent Schwartze served overseas with the Army during World War II and was discharged at the rank of staff sergeant. In the years following his service, he was employed with Capital City Telephone Company and United Telephone Company until his retirement in 1982. Schwartze passed away on August 26, 2005. (Jane Frank.)

A lifelong resident of Jefferson City, James Schell, shown here in 1944, served as a surveyor with an Army field artillery battery during World War II. He earned four Bronze Stars for his service in locations throughout Europe. In the years following his discharge, Schell became the manager at Atlas Material Company, a position he kept until the business closed in the early 1980s. He later went into business with his family at Schell Construction and operated his own surveying company for many years. (Pat Schell.)

Wayne Maloney was serving with the Army Air Forces in Europe as a radioman and gunner when his B-17 bomber was shot down over Holland during World War II. He spent 18 months in prison camp Stalag 17-B, located near Krems, Austria, until the camp was liberated in May 1945. Maloney passed away in April 1965 and is buried in Arlington National Cemetery. (David Maloney.)

Frank V. Distler is pictured above in 1944 with his daughter Shirley and his wife, Rosaline. Distler was killed in action on April 5, 1945, while serving in Europe with the Army's 191st Tank Battalion, making him the 100th Cole County resident to lose his life during the war. Distler was buried in the Lorraine American Cemetery in St. Avold, France. (Larry Schepker.)

In 1943, approximately a month before his graduation from high school, Perry Coy received word from his local draft board to get his affairs in order. Coy participated in several major European campaigns during World War II, earning three Purple Hearts, a Bronze Star, and a Silver Star Medal. After the war, he established Coy's Fire & Safety Equipment Company, which he operated for 35 years. (Perry Coy.)

Army veteran Perry Coy (third from right) is seen above in a 2010 ceremony at the Missouri capitol at which Gov. Jay Nixon (far left) presented him with a French Legion of Honor Medal on behalf of the French government. Pictured in military uniform are members of the 2nd Ranger Battalion of St. Louis, a group of World War II reenactors. (Shawn C. Johnson.)

James Clardy enlisted in the Marine Corps in September 1946 and served stateside until his discharge in 1948. He was recalled to active duty during the Korean War and served at Camp Pendleton, California. He later joined the Missouri National Guard, of which he remained a full-time employee until his death in 1979, having risen to the rank of colonel. Clardy is pictured here in his Marine Corps uniform around 1948. (Almira Clardy.)

Formed in 1942, the Navy Seabees was established to meet the nation's demand for individuals in the construction and building trades who could also fight. Since World War II, the Seabees have served around the globe in virtually every conflict, building bases, roads, and runways in support of the war effort. Pictured above is one of three memorials in the state dedicated to the service of the Seabees over the years. This one, in the Jefferson City National Cemetery, was dedicated in 2013. (Shawn C. Johnson.)

Not yet 21 years of age, Elmer Frank had to have his mother's signature so that he could enlist in the Marine Corps in September 1942. After completion of his initial training, Frank was assigned to Marine Air Group 13. By the time of his discharge in November 1945, he had served in several locations throughout the South Pacific and earned two Bronze Stars. (Mary Frank.)

Elmer Frank, a truck and tractor driver, is pictured above on an M2 High-Speed Tractor while assigned to Marine Fighter Squadron 461, Marine Base Defense Group, in 1944. Several years after the war, Frank started Midwest Block Company, which he co-owned for 35 years. In 1987, he was elected Cole County treasurer, an office he held for 12 years. (Mary Frank.)

Inducted into the Army on September 22, 1944, at Jefferson Barracks, Edgar Frank received training in teletype maintenance at Chanute Field, Illinois. He was deployed to Japan as part of the occupational forces following the surrender of Japanese forces and was discharged from the service on November 9, 1946, at the rank of staff sergeant. Edgar Frank went on to complete a career with the US Postal Service. (Mary Frank.)

Inducted into the Army on January 21, 1942, Norbert Frank served in stateside locations such as Long Island and San Diego until his discharge on December 18, 1945. After completing his enlistment, Frank was employed by propane gas companies in Sedalia and Jefferson City, and he also farmed until his retirement in 1982. (Margaret Ann Gerling.)

A 1938 graduate of Jefferson City High School, John Ambrose worked as a messenger at a local bank before enlisting in the Army in December 1941. Assigned to the 1562nd Army Air Forces Base Unit, he was stationed at several locations in the Pacific, including New Guinea, where he served as an air transportation technician. Following his discharge in 1945, Ambrose returned to Jefferson City and his banking job. He retired from Exchange National Bank in 1982 as the vice president of the lending department. (Becky Ambrose.)

Drafted in 1944, shortly after completing his junior year of high school, Jack Matthews was inducted into the Army and served with Company G, 2nd Battalion, 314th Infantry Regiment. His company saw action in locations including Czechoslavakia, France, and Germany, and Matthews earned a Bronze Star and a Combat Infantry Badge. Following his discharge in 1946, he finished his senior year of school. He has remained active in veterans affairs throughout the years, including service with the Missouri Veterans Commission from 1992 to 2000. (Jack Matthews.)

Dr. Robert H. King and his wife, Jean, are shown in their wedding photograph from 1949. Dr. King was drafted into the Army in 1942 and was stationed at Camp Van Dorn, Mississippi. While at the camp, King began working for the base chaplain and helped out at the base hospital. King was discharged from the service in August 1943 after he was found unfit for service due to an eye injury he sustained as a child. He later graduated seminary school and served in several capacities with the Lutheran Church, eventually becoming the second vice president of the Lutheran Church–Missouri Synod. (Robert King.)

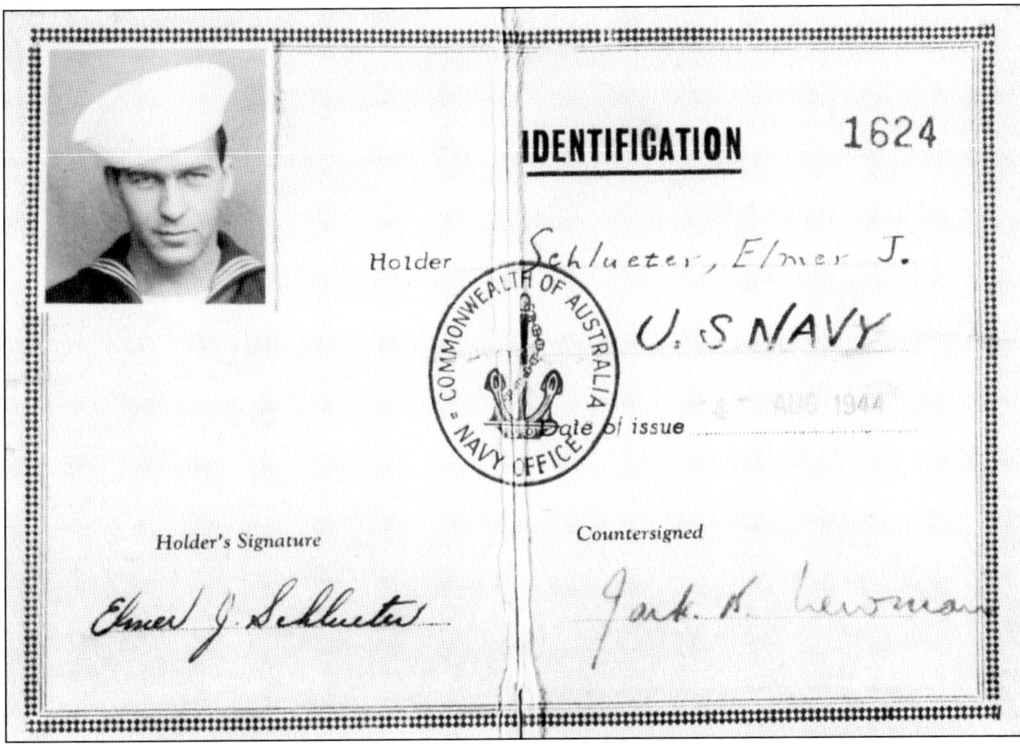

Enlisting in the Navy in 1942, Elmer Schlueter (above) helped decode Japanese messages during World War II and was stationed in Hawaii, New Guinea, Australia, Washington, DC, and Arlington, Virginia. He was recalled to active duty during the Korean War and served with the Armed Forces Security Agency in Virginia. In 1982, he retired from the Missouri Public Service Commission as the chief accountant after 36 years of service. This is the identification issued to Schlueter while he was stationed in Australia in 1944. (Jim Schlueter.)

Emylou Keith enlisted in the Army Nurse Corps in 1944 and was placed as nurse in charge of one of the wards at the former O'Reilly Army Hospital in Springfield, Missouri, during World War II. (Emylou Keith.)

Bill Amick enlisted in the Navy on June 19, 1942, at St. Louis, and he went on to complete gunnery school at Chicago. He became a qualified pointer and trainer on numerous different types of guns and served in the Pacific aboard several ships during the war. Amick was discharged in 1946 and worked as a journeyman electrician for 25 years with the International Brotherhood of Electrical Workers. He then started Bill Amick Electric Company, which he owned for another 25 years. (Charlotte Dewrock.)

Upon his graduation from the University of Missouri in 1941, William Bushman entered the Navy as an ensign. Following his initial training in radar, he was assigned to the light cruiser USS *St. Louis*. He served aboard the ship during several engagements, including the Battle of Kolombangara, during which a torpedo blew the bow off of the vessel. After the war, he went to work for the Westinghouse Corporation at locations in St. Louis, Kansas City, and Staunton, Virginia. Bushman passed away in 2009. (Bill Bushman.)

Gilbert Schanzmeyer enlisted in the Army Air Forces in 1943. Here, he poses next to one of the AT-6s with which he trained to become a pilot. In 1945, he received his commission and became qualified to fly the B-25 Mitchell, a twin-engine bomber. The Japanese surrender ended World War II only days after Schanzmeyer completed his aviation training. (Courtesy of Gilbert Schanzmeyer.)

The Schanzmeyer brothers pose for a group photograph in their respective military uniforms in 1952. They are, from left to right, Gilbert (Army Air Forces), Joe "Bud" (Army), Bernard (Army), and Pat (Army Air Forces). (Gilbert Schanzmeyer.)

Grayson Burmeister is seen here in 1944 while stationed at Camp Pendleton, California. Burmeister served overseas during World War II. After leaving the service in 1945, he returned to Jefferson City, where he spent many years in the automobile business. He was appointed as the supervisor of the Motor Vehicle Registration Unit at the Missouri Department of Revenue in 1970. Burmeister passed away in 1989 at age 71. (Tom Burmeister.)

Donald Martin Brucks, pictured here in 1943 at the age of 19, served in the Navy during World War II, and, later, in the Coast Guard. After the war, he returned to Jefferson City, where he operated Don Brucks Cities Service, located on Highway 50 at Dix Road. In later years, Brucks operated dealerships selling automobiles and boats and renting equipment such as trailers. (Diane Brucks McDonald.)

Three

Korea, Vietnam, and the Cold War

Pvt. Weldon Frey was drafted into the Army in 1952, when he was 21 years old. He trained as a tank operator at Fort Knox, Kentucky, before deploying to Korea in the summer of 1953. This photograph was taken about 1952. (Weldon Frey.)

While stationed with the 1st Cavalry Division in Korea, Weldon Frey became the commander of two M-24 tanks. Here, he poses with an M-24. (Weldon Frey.)

Wesley Godsy was a career military man. Toward the latter part of his time in the service, Godsy was assigned to the Reserve Officer Training Corps (ROTC) program at Lincoln University. After retiring from the service, he worked for Jefferson City's health department and housing authority, from which he retired in 1987. Godsy was a well-decorated veteran, having earned a Silver Star Medal, a Bronze Star, and two Purple Hearts. He is seen here while serving in Korea in 1951 as a reconnaissance sergeant with the 73rd Heavy Tank Battalion. (Martin Godsy.)

Bernard Schanzmeyer believed he would be drafted during World War II, but the war ended before that became a reality. Instead, he was drafted into the Army during the Korean War and spent several months in combat. Schanzmeyer is seen here while home on leave in 1952. (Bernard Schanzmeyer.)

Bernard Schanzmeyer (below, first row, far right) served as a squad leader while assigned to G Company, 19th Infantry Regiment, 24th Infantry Division, during the Korean War. While in combat, he was shot through the helmet by the enemy and was fortunate that the bullet missed his skull. On a separate occasion, he was wounded by shrapnel from an enemy mortar, but the injury was treated at an aid station. After the war, Schanzmeyer returned to mid-Missouri, where he owned car dealerships with his brothers. (Bernard Schanzmeyer.)

Bud Redel (right) receives a Purple Heart at a naval hospital in Japan in 1951. Redel enlisted in the Marine Corps in 1948 and was sent to Korea in 1950, participating in the Battle of Inchon. He later suffered from severe frostbite while serving in the Chosin Reservoir, narrowly avoiding having his feet amputated. Redel spent several months in hospitals recovering from his injuries and was discharged from the military in July 1952. (Bud Redel.)

The Missouri National Guard Headquarters, seen here in the 1950s, was located on the south side of the state capitol grounds, facing High Street. It had previously served as a federal courthouse and post office. (Museum of Missouri Military History.)

This photograph of the former headquarters building shows the names of other organizations housed in the facility, including the 735th Ordnance Battalion and subordinate units. (Museum of Missouri Military History.)

Missouri National Guardsmen take a break from their duties to play a game of table tennis in one of the rooms inside of the former headquarters building. (Museum of Missouri Military History.)

A 1948 graduate of St. Peter's High School, Paul Diemler enlisted in the Air Force in August 1950 and later served as a clerk with the 28th Strategic Reconnaissance Wing Heavy, located at Rapid City Air Force Base in South Dakota. Diemler passed away in 1968 at just 39 years of age. (Paula Diemler Volkart.)

In 1960, Cole County sheriff Horace Debo (below, center, in bow tie), in cooperation with 10 former Marines, established the Sheriff's Auxiliary. The Marines are seen here posing with Debo. The auxiliary was later expanded and organized into the sheriff patrol following the election of Wyman Basinger (second from right) as sheriff in 1968. The group volunteered its time to the sheriff's department and assisted in patrolling the county's roads and apprehending escaped prisoners. (Central Missouri Detachment, Marine Corps League.)

In the late 1940s, World War II veterans who were members of the local Veterans of Foreign Wars post formed a mortuary team that not only provided final honors at the funerals of their fallen comrades, but also participated in community events. The team dissolved in the late 1980s after many of its members passed away or were physically unable to continue their voluntary service. Here, members of the original mortuary team march in a parade on High Street in the 1960s. (Harold Markway.)

In 2001, members of Veterans of Foreign Wars Post 1003 formed an honor guard from the ashes of the mortuary team that had dissolved nearly two decades earlier. The honor guard now works cooperatively with the Missouri Funeral Honors Program to help provide military funeral honors for local deceased veterans. The honor guard is pictured here in their uniforms on October 16, 2011, in recognition of the team's 10-year anniversary. (Rowland Doerhoff.)

Steve Sampson enlisted in the Navy in 1963, where he was introduced to nuclear technologies while serving aboard submarines. This photograph was taken in Groton, Connecticut, in 1971, the year he left the Navy. (Steve Sampson.)

Sampson served two North Atlantic tours on board the USS *Henry Stimson* (below), a nuclear-powered ballistic missile submarine. He later used his Navy-acquired skills when he went to work at the Callaway Nuclear Plant near Fulton, Missouri. He retired as a shift manager at the facility in 2004. (Steve Sampson.)

Drafted into the Army in 1951, Bob Kettler served 17 months in country during the Korean War. Most of his time was spent as part of a team of investigators working to curb theft by local Koreans hired to assist the military. (Bob Kettler.)

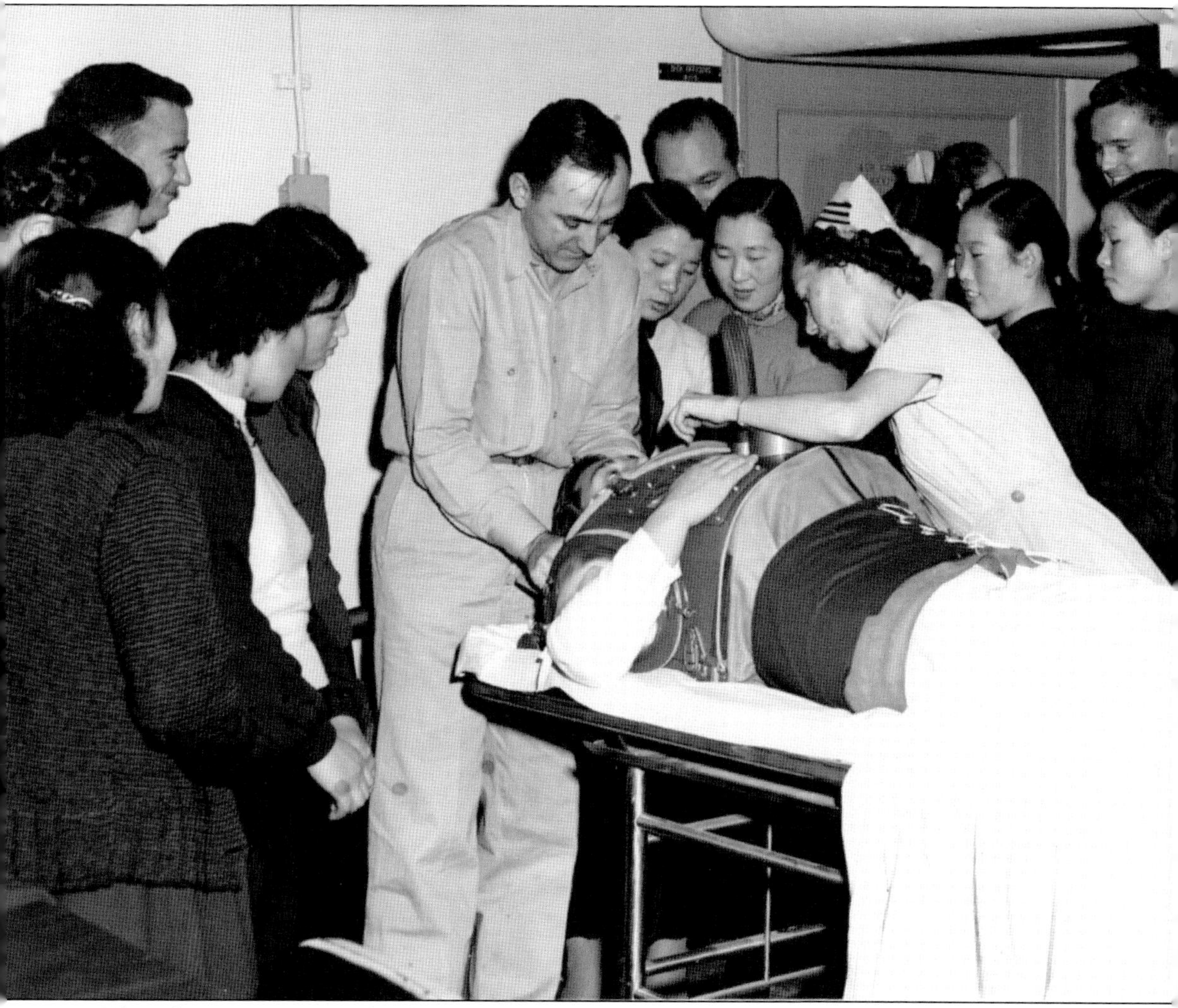

Though serving as a medical equipment repairman at the time, Bill McAnany was assigned additional duties while serving on the USS *Repose* in 1953, such as demonstrating the use of a portable iron lung to student nurses from a Korean hospital, as seen here. The ship anchored in Inchon Bay and treated injuries and illnesses during the Korean War. The ship also made regular trips to a naval hospital in Japan to transport for treatment service members who had more serious injuries. (Bill McAnany.)

William "Bill" Frank was inducted into the Army on January 9, 1951, and was stationed at Fort Sill, Oklahoma, after completing his initial training. He served two years on active duty and was then transferred to the Army Reserve, where he remained until his discharge on October 10, 1956. He owned and operated Frank's Barbershop in Florissant, Missouri, until his retirement. (Mary Frank.)

Army veteran Charlie Kuensting served 16 months in country during the Korean War. He was initially trained as an artilleryman but later volunteered to serve in the motor pool. He poses here with a trailer he converted into a generator using a Jeep motor while stationed in Korea. (Charlie Kuensting.)

Members of the community attend the 1957 ground-breaking for a new National Guard armory on St. Mary's Boulevard. The construction was authorized under Public Law 783, a new armory construction program that led to new facilities throughout the United States. In the distance is the Missouri River bridge (now the southbound span), completed two years prior to this event. (Museum of Missouri Military History.)

This is the site of the new Jefferson City Armory as it appeared when construction began in 1957. The site overlooks the area that would later become the Highway 50/Highway 54 interchange. Note the water tower in the background. (Museum of Missouri Military History.)

The completed Jefferson City Armory is seen above in July 1958. In later years, a second story was added to the building, and blue siding was attached to the exterior, lending the structure the nickname Blue Armory. It is one of the first identifiable landmarks motorists see as they cross the Missouri River into Jefferson City. (Museum of Missouri Military History.)

Samuel "Sam" Gearhart was a recruiter for the Marine Corps in Jefferson City in the 1960s. Though he was raised in Pennsylvania and spent much of his career in other locations, including Virginia, Indiana, and Kentucky, Gearhart moved back to Jefferson City after his retirement from the Marines in 1970, believing it to be a good area to raise a family. He is seen here around 1949. (Robin Smith.)

With a desire to see the world, Ruby Moses enlisted in the Marine Corps in 1951 and served at the American embassy in Germany. After leaving the service, Moses went on to complete a career with the US Postal Service. (Sallie Moses Jacobs.)

Following in the footsteps of her older sister, Jacque Moses enlisted in the Marine Corps in 1952. She served in communications at the Marine Headquarters in Washington, DC. She was married while in the service and, after her discharge in 1954, became a homemaker, raising five sons and a daughter. (Sallie Moses Jacobs.)

Sgt. Ruby Moses of Jefferson City was among the first of a group of female Marines selected for European assignment. She traveled to Germany in November 1952 as part of a two-year tour of duty. Moses is in the first row, second from left, wearing her hat. (Sallie Moses Jacobs.)

Enlisting in the Marine Corps in 1944, Tom Stuckenschneider became a field artillery crewman and saw combat in the Pacific, including during the occupation of China, from September 1945 to March 1946. Stuckenschneider, discharged in April 1946, was recalled to active duty during the Korean War and was later discharged from Camp Pendleton, California, due to a physical disability. Stuckenschneider is pictured here in 1951. (Eleanor Stuckenschneider.)

Donald Jennings enlisted in the Navy during the Korean War. After completing his basic training, Jennings served in Washington, DC, at the National Security Information Center. He later went to work for the IBM office in Jefferson City, retiring in 1992 with 38 years of service to the company. (Carrie McIlwain.)

After participating in the Reserve Officer Training Corps while attending Lincoln University, Richard "Dick" Cramer was commissioned a second lieutenant in the Army following his graduation in 1952. Cramer is pictured here boarding the train in Hermann in 1953, on his way to the West Coast and his eventual service with the 143rd Field Artillery during the Korean War. Several years after his return from the war, Cramer and his wife opened Cramer Decorating Shop in Jefferson City. (Patsy Cramer.)

Volunteering for the Army draft, James Kellerman (right) completed cryptology training at Camp Gordon, Georgia, and was deployed to Korea, where he spent 16 months at a compound situated on the 38th parallel. Working out of a tent with a dozen other soldiers, he coded, decoded, and delivered messages. In December 1955, he was discharged from the service. Kellerman went on to earn his doctoral degree by utilizing his GI Bill educational benefits. (James Kellerman.)

A 1960 graduate of Jefferson City High School, Lt. Laughton Smith attended the Naval Academy and was serving on board the USS *Scorpion* submarine when he and 98 other sailors were lost at sea on May 22, 1968. The circumstances leading to the loss of the submarine are still uncertain. It is suspected that mechanical failure may have been the cause. (Sallie Moses Jacobs.)

Ed Irwin enlisted in the Navy shortly after graduating high school in 1962. He went on to enjoy a 20-year military career, much of it spent on or around submarines. Irwin went to work for the Callaway Nuclear Plant following his discharge. He retired in 2008 with 24 years of service to the company. (Ed Irwin.)

Shown here is the launching of the USS *Archerfish* (SSN-678), a Sturgeon-class attack submarine, in January 1971. Local veteran Ed Irwin served a two-year stint on board the submarine and was present for the launch. (Ed Irwin.)

Uel Smith spent his entire Cold War–era service aboard submarines, first with the USS *Cubera*, a diesel-powered submarine built during World War II. Smith later transferred to the USS *Growler*, on which he remained until his discharge in 1960. He then went to work for Cowley Distributing in Jefferson City, remaining with the company until his retirement in 2004. Here, Smith poses in his enlistment photograph from 1956. (Uel Smith.)

With a "grease gun" slung over his shoulder, Navy veteran Tom Ward is seen here in 1969, posing with children in a South Vietnamese village. He was providing security for a team of doctors and combat medics treating Vietnamese civilians as part of a humanitarian initiative called the Medical Civic Action Program. (Tom Ward.)

Jim Carter deployed to Vietnam in 1967 and was assigned as a chaplain with the 52nd Combat Aviation Battalion, located on Camp Holloway, near Pleiku. Leaving active service in 1972, he pastored at several churches and served as chaplain for medical centers in both Missouri and Texas, eventually retiring in 2009 from St. Mary's Medical Center in Jefferson City. Here, Chaplain Carter visits with children at an orphanage near Pleiku, Vietnam. (Jim Carter.)

On September 16, 1966, while serving in Vietnam with Company D, 1st Battalion, 4th Marines, Rick Fechtel (left) was shot through the jaw by enemy troops. While trying to locate his fellow Marines, he was wounded a second time when an enemy bullet struck him below the shoulder. A little while later, while being evacuated on a helicopter, Fechtel was wounded a third and final time when he was shot in the buttocks. The Purple Heart recipient later recovered from his wounds and returned to Jefferson City, where he completed a career with the US Postal Service. Fechtel is seen here with fellow Marine Mark Ferguson, who was killed in action on September 17, 1966. (Rick Fechtel.)

Steven P. Amick (above, center) enlisted in the Marine Corps in 1965 along with his friends Ron Saucier (left) and Roger Weider. A few months after completing radio relay school, Amick volunteered for service in Vietnam. He was assigned to Headquarters Company, 5th Marines, located on Hill 35, just 15 miles north of Chu Lai. While in country, Amick was stricken with malaria and spent 38 days in the hospital. After his discharge in 1967, he worked as an electrician and later retired from state government. (Steven P. Amick.)

Steven Brown served in the Marine Corps from 1966 to 1969 as a radio operator and cryptographer. He is seen here in 1969 while stationed on the aircraft carrier USS *Coral Sea* (CVA-43). Brown's duties included the interception of several types of signal intelligence, which were then reported to the National Security Agency in Fort Meade, Maryland, for analysis. (Steve Brown.)

Sam Gearhart served during the Korean War and, in 1968, deployed to Vietnam. After his return to Jefferson City in the early 1970s, Gearhart became active in the Marine Corps League, which was named in his honor in 2006. Gearhart died in 2005 and was laid to rest at Arlington National Cemetery. Staff Sergeant Gearhart is pictured here in 1954 while serving in Quantico, Virginia. (Robin Smith.)

Below, William "Skip" Rich (left) poses for a photograph with actor John Wayne in 1966 while stationed at Da Nang Air Base with the 1st Marine Air Wing. Rich, a 1963 graduate of Jefferson City High School, served in Vietnam from May 1966 to December 1967. He later served for 30 years as the Cole County collector. Rich retired from the Missouri National Guard in 2005 at the rank of command sergeant major after 25 years of service. (Samuel F. Gearhart Detachment, Marine Corps League.)

David Mauldin poses in front of his "hooch" in Nha Trang, Vietnam, around 1970. Mauldin was drafted into the Army and served a tour in Vietnam with the 1st Field Force Headquarters. He was discharged from the Army in 1971 and joined the Missouri National Guard the following year, retiring in 2008 at the rank of sergeant major. (David Mauldin.)

This photograph was taken in December 1969 at a forward observation post several hundred yards from "LZ Baldy/Hill 55" in Vietnam. Sgt. Donley "Dan" Amick, a 1966 graduate of Jefferson City High School, enlisted in the Marine Corps in 1968. He served in the field artillery with the 3rd Battalion, 11th Marines, in Vietnam from 1969 to 1970. (Dan Amick.)

Vietnam veterans and brothers Dan (right) and Steve Amick help present singer and actress Ann-Margret with the annual Silver Star Families of America Commendation Award in a 2011 ceremony in Branson, Missouri. Dan Amick saw Ann-Margret perform in 1969 during a USO Christmas performance in Da Nang, Vietnam, while he was serving in the Marine Corps. (Shawn C. Johnson.)

A 1963 graduate of Helias High School, Hal Dulle (above) attended college prior to enlisting in the Marine Corps in 1966. He began his military career in motor transport, but later completed administrative school and was deployed to Southeast Asia for 18 months, spending time in both Vietnam and Guam. Following his discharge, Dulle finished his bachelor's degree in economics at Lincoln University in 1972. Here, he attends boot camp at the Marine Corps Recruit Depot in San Diego in March 1966. (Hal Dulle.)

Drafted into military service in 1967, Don Hentges completed his initial training with the Army the following year and deployed to Vietnam, where he served as a rifleman with the 101st Airborne. While on patrol during his deployment, Hentges was injured when a member of his squad tripped a booby trap. Hentges's injuries earned him a Purple Heart and led to his medical discharge from the Army in June 1969. (Don Hentges.)

Army veteran Don Hentges has served as president of the Jefferson City Veterans Council for several years. Here, Hentges (right) receives a Silver Star Banner from Missouri governor Jay Nixon in 2011 in recognition of the injuries he received under combat conditions. (Shawn C. Johnson.)

While serving a 13-month tour in Vietnam with the Marine Corps, Ron Saucier (right) spent several months with a Combined Action Platoon in the Vietnamese village of Tuy Loan. The platoon, consisting of 10 Marines and a Navy corpsman, was part of an effort to win the "hearts and minds" of the Vietnamese people by living among them and providing protection and basic medical care. Here, Saucier poses with a member of the Popular Forces after returning from a patrol in December 1966. (Ron Saucier.)

Enlisting in the Army in 1971, Warren Krech was transferred to Kagnew Station in Asmara, Ethiopia (now Eritrea), where he worked as an entertainment specialist in special services. In addition to his duties of managing the base swimming pool, Krech learned the basics of broadcasting while in the Army and even hosted a television show for the children of soldiers serving on the base. Krech's character Crater Eddie is pictured above in the early 1970s on the set of his Saturday morning children's program. After leaving the service, Krech earned his degree from the University of Minnesota and has worked for local radio outlets since 1984. (Warren Krech.)

Tyronne Allen served in the Air Force from 1967 to 1971. He deployed to South Korea in 1968 as part of Operation Combat Fox, the US response to North Korean forces capturing the USS *Pueblo*. He later volunteered for service during the Vietnam War and was deployed to an air base in Thailand, where he worked in support of B-52 bombing missions in Vietnam. In 2009, Allen retired as the library director for the Missouri Supreme Court. (Tyronne Allen.)

A 1959 graduate of Jefferson City High School, 1st Lt. Guy Hackman was an aerial artillery observer with the Army, serving in Vietnam with the 1st Infantry Division from 1965 to 1966. Hackman, posing here beside a Bell H13 helicopter, performed target acquisition and directed artillery strikes using aerial observation, in addition to directing ship-to-shore naval gunfire on targets along the coast of Vietnam. In June 1966, he was awarded a Distinguished Flying Cross for heroism while participating in aerial flight. (Guy Hackman.)

David Maloney is seen here as a Marine Corps recruit in 1959. He served four years active duty with the Corps, from 1959 to 1963, and was stationed at the Marine Corps Air Station at Kaneohe Bay, Hawaii, where he helped issue driver's licenses and trained his fellow Marines on the operation of various types of military equipment. In the years following his military service, Maloney retired from the Jefferson City Housing Authority after 27 years of service as a maintenance supervisor and mechanical engineer. (David Maloney.)

A 1966 graduate of Jefferson City High School, Larry Matthews attended Lincoln University and, in 1971, graduated from the University of Missouri–Columbia, where he received his military commission through the ROTC program. He served for 30 years with the Army in locations such as Korea, Hawaii, Bahrain, and Saudi Arabia. (Nancy Fesler.)

Capt. Larry Matthews (center) speaks with Rep. Richard Ichord Jr. (right), who was part of a delegation visiting troops at military posts in Hawaii. This photograph was taken in 1980, while Matthews was stationed at Schofield Barracks, Hawaii. (Nancy Fesler.)

Capt. Bill Stine (right) receives an Air Force Commendation Medal in 1982 in recognition of his work while stationed at Hanscom Air Force Base in Massachusetts. Stine enlisted in the Air Force in 1967 and spent the next two decades working at various locations throughout the United States with emerging technologies, such as the communication systems aboard Minuteman missiles. (William Stine.)

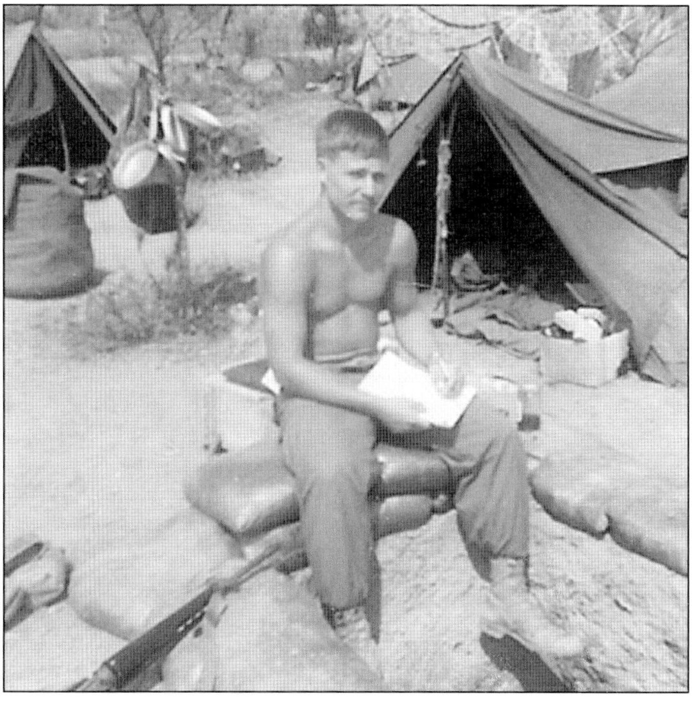

While growing up, James M. McIlwain attended both parochial and public schools locally, graduating in 1966 from Jefferson City High School. He soon joined the Marine Corps, serving over a year in Vietnam with the 1st Marine Division. Participating in several operations, McIlwain was wounded by an enemy explosive device during Operation Ford and was awarded the Purple Heart. Leaving the service in 1969, he was employed by United Telephone Company. After being laid off, he went to work for Capitol Concrete, eventually retiring as a union concrete driver. (Carrie McIlwain.)

Drafted into the Army in April 1965, Robert Verslues finished boot camp at Fort Leonard Wood, Missouri, and armor training at Fort Knox, Kentucky. He was then sent to Germany, where he was assigned to an armored unit as a tank driver. He eventually worked his way up to tank commander. He remained in Germany until his discharge in April 1967. Here, Verslues participates in tank maneuvers in Wildflecken, Germany. (Rosie Verslues.)

On June 14, 2008, the Jefferson City Public Schools (JCPS) Alumni Association presented a veterans memorial listing the names of all JCPS students who died while in service to the nation. The memorial, representing those fallen from World War I onward, is located in the lobby of the Marvin Fleming Field House. (Sallie Moses Jacobs.)

The Museum of Missouri Military History, located on the grounds of the Missouri National Guard Headquarters, opened in 1999. It was originally located in a building that was once the housing unit for inmates working the farm at the local prison in the early 1900s. (Shawn C. Johnson.)

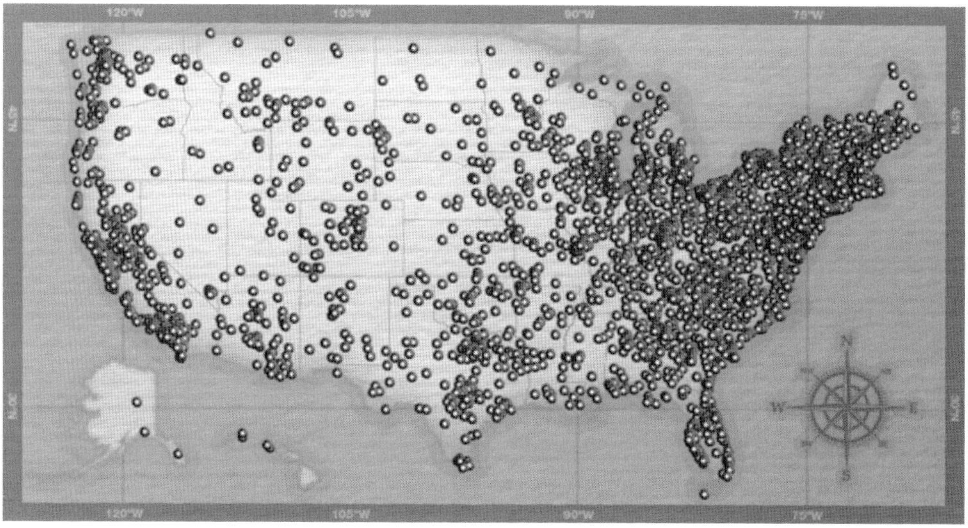